GOOD TO BE GREEN

# Let's Walk to School

Written by DEBORAH CHANCELLOR

Illustrated by DIANE EWEN

A story about why it's important to walk more.

WAYLAND

www.waylandbooks.co.uk

"Time to go!" said Mum.

Tom was hiding.
"I don't like school,"
he said. "I'd rather stay
at home."

3

"I can't leave you here," said Mum.

"I've got to go to work."

4

Tom pulled a face.

"I'll give you a lift," said Mum.

Tom got dressed in a hurry.
He got in the car and Mum
started the engine.

On short trips we can walk or ride a
bike, skateboard or scooter to save **fuel** and cut
**pollution**. This is good for the **environment**.

Soon they were stuck in a traffic jam.

Tom closed the car window.

"The air smells terrible!" he said.

"That's because of the traffic fumes," said Mum.

Traffic **fumes** pollute the air we breathe. Factories, **power stations** and dairy farms, through cow burps, also add to the problem of air pollution.

"It's so hot!" said Tom.

"Our summers are getting hotter," said Mum.

"Air pollution is heating up the Earth
and it's called **global warming**."
Tom didn't like the sound of this.

"Let's walk to school tomorrow," said Mum.
"Walking is good for the environment
because it doesn't make any pollution."
"But it's much too hot to walk!" said Tom.

Pollution rises into the Earth's **atmosphere**, trapping some of the Sun's rays. This warms up the Earth's surface, changing our weather patterns.

13

So the next day, Mum drove Tom to school again.

There was a big thunderstorm.

"Let's walk to school tomorrow," said Mum.

"But it's much too wet to walk!" said Tom.

Global warming is slowly changing our climate, bringing extreme weather around the world, such as **droughts**, storms and **floods**.

So the next day, Mum drove Tom to school again.

They got stuck in the worst traffic jam, ever.

"I've had enough of this!" said Mum.

"No excuses – you're walking to school tomorrow!"

"I'm going to take the train to work," said Mum.

"And you can walk, whatever the weather."

You can help reduce traffic on the roads by walking or taking **public transport**, for example using trains, buses and trams.

The next day, Mum left the car at home.

She went to work by train and Tom set off for

school on foot.

Walking and cycling keeps us fit and healthy. It makes our muscles strong and is good for our hearts. It keeps our brains active, too!

At first, Tom wasn't very happy. But then he met a girl called Fen on the way. The walk was fun.

"Let's walk to school tomorrow," said Fen.

Tom liked the sound of this.

Mum got home from work early.

"My train was so quick!" she said.

"How was school?"

"It was fun," said Tom. "And from now on,
I'm going to walk to school every day!"

# Quiz time

Which of these things are true?

Read the book again to find out!

*(Cover up the answers on page 27.)*

1. Air pollution is only caused by traffic jams.

2. Air pollution is bad for the environment.

3. Our climate is changing because of global warming.

4. Public transport adds to all the traffic on the roads.

5. Walking is bad for you, because it makes you tired.

# Answers

1. **False:** Traffic fumes are not the only cause of air pollution. Factories, power stations and cow burps add to the problem. *(See page 9)*

2. **True:** Air pollution rises into the atmosphere, trapping some of the Sun's rays. This warms the Earth's surface, changing weather patterns. *(See page 13)*

3. **True:** Global warming is heating up the Earth. This is changing our climate and bringing extreme weather, such as floods and droughts. *(See page 15)*

4. **False:** If more people took trains, buses and trams, there would be fewer cars on the roads, and less traffic. *(See page 19)*

5. **False:** Walking and cycling keeps you fit and healthy. It is good for the environment, too. *(See page 21)*

# Get active

- In the story, Tom and his mum change the way they do things to help the environment – Tom starts walking to school and Mum takes the train to work. Do you make any unnecessary car journeys? Can you think of another way to make those journeys?

- Ask an adult to take you on a bus or train ride. Take some photos and put together a photo story of your trip when you get home. You could add speech bubbles to make your story more fun to read!

- Ask your friends: Who walks to school? Who goes by bus? Who goes by train? Who gets a lift in a car? Make a bar chart to show how many people do each activity. What is the most popular way to get to school?

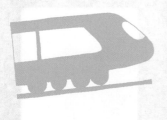

- Air pollution adds to the problems of global warming and climate change. Look out for stories in the news about extreme weather around the world, for example hurricanes, floods and droughts. Make a collage of dangerous weather events that may be caused by global warming.

# Glossary

| | |
|---|---|
| **atmosphere** | the air around the Earth |
| **climate** | the pattern of weather over a long period of time |
| **drought** | a long time without rain, leading to a water shortage |
| **environment** | the world around us |
| **floods** | large amounts of water overflowing into areas that are normally dry |
| **fuel** | material (such as gas or oil) burned for heat or power |
| **fumes** | smoky gas that comes from burning engine fuel |
| **global warming** | the rising temperature of the Earth's surface, caused by air pollution |
| **pollution** | harmful chemicals that make a place or thing dirty |
| **power station** | place where electric power is generated and sent out |
| **public transport** | ways of getting about that many people can use at the same time, such as buses and trains |

# A note about sharing this book

The GOOD TO BE GREEN series provides a starting point for further discussion on important environmental issues, such as pollution, climate change and endangered wildlife. The topics considered in each book are relevant to all, children and adults alike.

# Let's Walk to School

This story explores, in a familiar context, some issues surrounding the problem of air pollution. *Let's Walk to School* contains practical suggestions for how to reduce air pollution, for example by choosing to walk rather than travel by car on short trips, and by using buses or trains for longer journeys. The information panels in the book also cover the wider issue of global warming and climate change, explaining in simple terms what causes this problem, and the effect it has around the world.

The story and non-fiction elements in *Let's Walk to School* encourage the reader to conclude that we should all walk or cycle, when possible, or use public transport, as this helps to reduce air pollution and also to save fuel.

# How to use the book

The story is designed for adults to share with either an individual child or a group of children, and as a starting point for discussion. The book provides visual support to raise confidence in children who are starting to read on their own. Repetition is used to reinforce understanding, for example the phrase 'let's walk to school tomorrow' is found at points throughout the book, building familiarity. The positive ending of the story is emphasised when the earlier sentence, 'Tom didn't like the sound of this', is changed to 'Tom liked the sound of this.'

The story introduces vocabulary relevant to the theme of air pollution, such as: *'atmosphere'*, *'climate'*, *'drought'*, *'engine'*, *'environment'*, *'factories'*, *'fuel'*, *'fumes'*, *'global warming'*, *'pollution'*, *'power station'*, *'public transport'*.

There is also an index at the back of the book, a standard feature of non-fiction books. Encourage the children to use the index when you are talking about the book -

for example, ask them to use the index to find the pages that describe global warming (*pages 11 and 15*). This useful research skill can be practised at an early age. It is important that children know that information can be found in books as well as searched for on the Internet with a responsible adult.

## Before reading the story

Pick a time to read when you and the children are relaxed and can take time to share the story together. Before you start reading, look at the illustrations and discuss what the book may be about.

## After reading, talk about the book

Discuss the story together, perhaps asking the following questions:

- Why doesn't Tom want to walk to school? (*see pages 2-3, 12-13, 14-15*)
- Why is the drive to school so slow? (*see pages 8-9*)
- Why does the air smell so bad? (*see pages 8-9*)
- Why is walking good for the environment? (*see pages 12-13*)
- Why does Mum decide to stop driving Tom to school? (*see pages 16-17*)
- How does Mum get to work instead? (*see pages 18-19*)
- What happens when Tom walks to school? (*see pages 22-23*)

Look at the information panels, then talk together about air pollution. You could ask the following questions:

- Why is it good to walk or cycle on a short trip? (*see pages 7 and 21*)
- What causes air pollution? (*see page 9*)
- Why is air pollution bad for the environment? (*see page 13*)
- What is happening because of global warming? (*see page 15*)
- How can you help to cut the amount of traffic on the roads? (*see page 19*)

Do the quiz together (*see pages 26-27*). It may help to re-read the information panels if the children's answers are wrong or if they just seem to be guessing!

# Index

First published in Great Britain in 2019
by Wayland
Copyright © Hodder and Stoughton, 2019

Editor: Sarah Peutrill
Designer: Cathryn Gilbert

ISBN (HB): 978 1 5263 0888 7
ISBN (PB): 978 1 5263 0889 4

Printed in China

Wayland, an imprint of
Hachette Children's Group
Part of Hodder and Stoughton
Carmelite House
50 Victoria Embankment
London EC4Y 0DZ

An Hachette UK Company
www.hachette.co.uk
www.hachettechildrens.co.uk

FSC
www.fsc.org

MIX
Paper from
responsible sources
FSC® C104740